The Happiness Book For Men

A Man's Guide To Happiness!

Mike Duffy

Copyright © 2014 Happiness Publishing, LLC
All images courtesy
of 123 RF.com
All rights reserved.
ISBN-13:978-0692315378
ISBN-10:0692315373

Dedication

I dedicate this book to my incredible family including my beautiful wife Shannon, my gorgeous daughter, Kendall, my wonderful son, Michael and the greatest dad ever, Michael J. Duffy.

Author's Note

This book is designed to put you in a happy state to help you learn and retain the wisdom of the top happiness experts in the world. Most books go unread because they are boring. I used funny pictures of English and French bulldogs to keep you turning the page to see what's next. The book is easy to read on purpose. It is specifically created to help men live a happier, more fulfilling and joyful life. My purpose in life is to make others happy and share all that I have learned about happiness. This book is the result of my over 29 years of researching happiness. Enjoy and be happy!

Have Good Relationships

I asked Harvard professor Daniel Gilbert if he could give me a tip that someone could use to increase their happiness. He said, "If someone asked me for the one nugget of wisdom that comes out of the scientific literature on happiness, my answer would be "have good relationships." We are the most social animals on our planet, and it is not surprising that our happiness depends mightily on the number and strength of our ties to other people. If you asked most people if they'd rather lose their friends or their eyesight, they'd choose the former. Bad choice. Blind people are perfectly happy people. Friendless people are not."

Make The Magic

Don't wait for life to somehow be fun and exciting. In my house, I am in charge of "making the magic." On Saturday mornings, if we don't have anything planned as a family, my wife and kids will say, "Make the magic, daddy!" I then go online for fun things to do and great places to go locally.

Seek Wisdom

Knowledge is important. Knowledge can give you the "How," but wisdom can give you the "Why." Sophocles said, "Wisdom is the supreme part of happiness."

Get a Massage

There are many benefits of a massage. Science shows that endorphins are released, stress is minimized and healing occurs. It is a great replacement for a food reward as well.

Live Life With Expectancy

Believe things will work in your favor. Expect things will go your way. If you don't believe you cannot succeed. St. Paul said, "I can do all things…"

Marry The Right Woman

Marry only for love. Looks will fade. Marry someone who is kind. Look for someone who is good to their parents. My mother used to tell me, "Show me someone who is good to their mother and I will show you a good person."

Travel

Travel will open your mind to all the possibilities that can occur if you apply yourself. It is a great way to see all the great creations that humans have made over the centuries. Visit inspiring places that you are interested in. Take a companion to deepen your relationship and have great conversations for years.

Let It Go!

Stop. Stop right now. Make a decision that whatever bad things happened in the past will remain there. Today is a new day and a new chance to make your life the greatest it can be.

Keep Learning

Take an adult education course at a local college in a course that you are interested in. Don't have the time? You can take online college courses for free. Keep learning, keep stretching and keep growing as a person.

Read

Reading opens your mind to every experience in the human condition. Read uplifting and inspiring books. My father is 81 and he reads a book a week. He is one of the happiest people that I know.

Put Your Wife First

Happy wife, happy life. Period. End of story. Ask any man married fifty years or more and he'll tell you the same thing. The more you make your wife feel special, the happier your marriage will be.

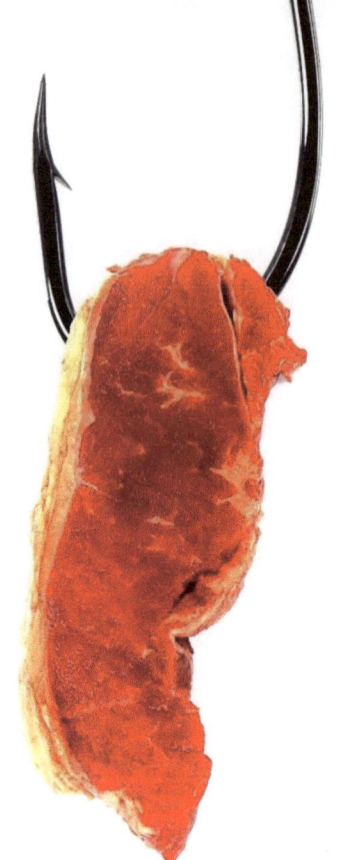

Don't Cheat!

Cheating on a loved one is a terrible thing to do. It may seem tempting at the time, but the effects are disastrous, especially to your reputation. Be a man of excellence.

Embrace the World With Open Arms

Treat your life like an adventure instead of a routine. Join clubs, charities and sports teams. Be open to all of the wonderful potential relationships and results that can occur on a daily basis.

Be Content With What You Have

Be on guard against the green-eyed monster of envy. There will always be people with more than you and less than you. Alfred Noble said, "Contentment is the only real wealth."

Be Enthusiastic!

Showing passion in words and body language is inspiring to others. Non-verbal communication represents the bulk of our communication, so stand up straight and smile. We need to "sell" our ideas, thoughts and emotions on a daily basis. Enthusiasm helps you close.

Have A Happy Heart

Always find the humor in everything, especially disappointments.
Proverbs 15:15 says,
For the despondent, every day brings trouble; for the happy heart, life is a continual feast.

Choose To Be Happy

Dr. Laura Delizonna is a professor at Stanford, a leader in the field of happiness and a Happiness Hall of Fame inductee. I took her wonderful course on happiness. Her research indicates that happiness is a choice. You must **choose** to be happy all through the day, no matter what life throws at you.

Never Give Up!

Regardless of countless failures, Thomas Edison never gave up in his quest for the light bulb. As a result, he lit the world. Anything worthwhile is worth fighting for. Be a man of great character and resilience.

Don't Wait For Happiness

I asked Shawn Achor, the author of *The Happiness Advantage* for some insights on happiness. He said, "Waiting for happiness decreases your success rates. Over a decade of my work in positive psychology with companies shows that happiness is a precursor to success, not merely the result of it. Most people think, if you work hard you will be successful and if you're successful then you'll be happy. But every time your brain hits a success, your brain moves the goal post of what "success" looks like, thwarting sustained happiness. But if you prioritize practicing positive habits in the present, every single business and educational outcome rises. Happy brains are 31% more productive, generate 37% higher sales, and are 40% more likely to receive a promotion. The greatest competitive advantage in the modern economy is a positive and engaged brain."

Be Social

Shawn Achor also stresses, "Do not abandon the greatest predictor of happiness. As I worked with Harvard students, I realized that many of them, when the stress level rose, they slowly divorced themselves from their social support networks (study breaks, hanging out with friends, extracurricular, intramurals). As they did so, their grades and happiness plummet. Social support is the greatest predictor of long-term happiness. There is a .7 correlation between social connection and happiness, which doesn't sound sexy but is significantly higher than the connection between smoking and cancer. And social connection is as predictive of how long you will live as obesity, high blood pressure and smoking. If you want to live longer, be happier and be more successful, when stress rises, double down and raise your social investment. You will reap the dividends of happiness and health the rest of your life."

Forgive

My friend, Dr. Fred Luskin is the best-selling author of *Forgive For Good.* He teaches a fantastic course on happiness at Stanford University and is a Happiness Hall Of Fame inductee. He believes that forgiveness is a key component of happiness. Grudges are like anchors that keep you stuck on the dock, while your dreamboat of happiness sails off into the sunset. Don't forget to forgive yourself, too!

Smile

Did you know that you can trick your mind into believing that it is happy by simply smiling? Smiling not only elevates your mood, but it also elevates those around you. People are apt to trust you more if you smile. More trust leads to more friendships and more friendships leads to more happiness. Are you seeing how this works yet?

Simplify!

Tal Ben-Shahar taught happiness courses at Harvard. He is the author of *Happier*. I asked Tal for advice for this book. He said, "Simplify! We are, generally, too busy, trying to squeeze in more and more activities into less and less time. Quantity influences quality, and we compromise on our happiness by trying to do too much. Knowing when to say 'no' to others often means saying 'yes' to ourselves."

Accept Your Humanity

Tal Ben-Shahar also told me, "Give yourself permission to be human. When we accept emotions -- such as fear, sadness, or anxiety -- as natural, we are more likely to overcome them. Rejecting our emotions, positive or negative, leads to frustration and unhappiness. We are a culture obsessed with pleasure and believe that the mark of a worthy life is the absence of discomfort; and when we experience pain, we take it to indicate that something must be wrong with us. In fact, there is something wrong with us if we don't experience sadness or anxiety at times--which are human emotions. The paradox is that when we accept our feelings--when we give ourselves the permission to be human and experience painful emotions--we are more likely to open ourselves up to positive emotions."

Say You Are Sorry

People need to know that you are regretful for the harm that you caused them. Telling them that you are sorry will let them heal and forgive you. This lets the relationship recover and move on. It takes a big man to admit to his mistakes.

Be Grateful

You are still on this side of the dirt. No matter how bad things get, you still have things to be grateful for. Count things like rational thought, existence, the gift of sight, the love of family and friends as a blessing. You have many more things than you don't have.

P+P=H

This is my happiness formula:
Purpose + Progress = Happiness. What is your purpose? We are not here to just be consumers. As you make progress in your purpose, you will be happy.

Have Faith

The majority of scientific studies have shown that people who have faith in God lead happier lives. Joining a faith community brings you in touch with like-minded people who can be there for you when times get rocky. I can tell you personally, that faith is a large component of my happiness.

Do Not Be Afraid

Fear and happiness cannot co-exist. Fear is one of the greatest roadblocks to happiness. Look back on your life. No matter what your troubles were, you got through. The future is no different. You will get through. Surrendering to fear makes you less effective at solving the problem that you are in. Push fear to the side and embrace happiness.

Find A Mentor

Find people that have "been there, done that" and are successful at whatever you are looking to improve at. They can shave years off of you trying to achieve your goals. Most people who have made it love to help others to the same level.

Be A Mentor

It is very fulfilling to help people arrive at the right destination. Older folks generally need help with computers. When you show them tips like "Control S" or help them get on Facebook, they have such an immediate reaction of joy. That will make your day better. Younger people need wise counsel when it comes to careers and love. Be the person that you wish you always had access to when you were younger. When you are older, maybe they will help you with your computer or anti-gravity boot questions.

Think Positive Thoughts

You cannot achieve a goal that you do not believe is doable. There would be no United States without George Washington's positive thoughts that he could overthrow British rule. He gambled all for his belief in a better life. You cannot be happy if you live a life of fear.

Enjoy And Celebrate Your Uniqueness

You are a precious commodity. There is only one of you. Stop trying to be everyone else and accept yourself. Not everyone will like you. The people that do like you are your real friends.

Be Kind

Use the acronym KLAP, which stands for Kindness, Love, And Patience, when you are speaking to someone. Mean words not only hurt the other person, they will come back to hurt you in the future. People avoid impatient people. Have a reputation of kindness and you will always be welcomed wherever you go. The strongest men are kind men.

See The Silver Lining

When you are going through a rough spot, it is hard to be excited about what good could come out of it. There is always something to learn from every experience, good and bad. Try to see the good.

Take Care Of Your Body

Your body is your temple. You must love yourself. Eating the wrong food, doing drugs, drinking too much, and not getting enough sleep will stall your true growth as a person. The mind-body connection cannot be overlooked when it comes to happiness.

Set The Right Goals

Noble goals, like serving and helping others, will lead to happiness. Change the world one person at a time. Be a force for good. Build a reputation as an honorable, loving man.

Be A Better Father

Be gentler and more patient with your children. Just when you think you cannot take any more questions about clouds and the sky, think of the acronym KLAP (kindness, love, and patience). Read to them more. Einstein said, "If you want your children to be intelligent, read them fairy tales. If you want them to be more intelligent, read them more fairy tales." Be the parent that you always wanted your parent to be.

Be A Better Child

No matter how bad or good your parents were to you, be better to them. Without them, you would not be here. Most parents tried their best. Don't carry grudges against your parents. Forgive them for their shortcomings. It will set you free. You will also set a great example for your children on how to take care of their parents. Do you see yet how goodness is a circle?

Schedule Fun

If you are married, have a regular date night. If it is Saturday at 5:30, I am on a date with my wife. If you have kids, have a family night or afternoon just devoted to fun. Life can be very busy. Do not surrender your precious life to the TV.

Shake Off The Negative

Hurt, anger, resentment, and regret are anchors that hold us back from our divine fate. Your true spirit yearns to soar and be free. Do not let these negative emotions nest in your soul. Shake them off and be free from the pain. They do not belong as a part of you. Refuse to be pulled down into the morass of depression. Use humor as a shield.

Watch What You Watch

Don't watch sad movies. When you walk out of a movie theater after watching a sad movie, do you feel great, inspired, and ready to take on life's challenges? Of course not! Watch more feel-good movies and comedies. Whatever you feed your mind will manifest itself in your life. Same thing goes for depressing music.

Laugh More

Go see a great comedian at a local comedy club. Watch more comedies on TV and at the movies. If you have satellite radio, they have channels devoted entirely to comedy. You can actually have a good belly laugh sitting in a traffic jam. Laughter releases endorphins and helps reduce stress hormones. It also strengthens your immune system.

Get A Good Night's Sleep

You can't take on the world if you are yawning at your desk. Use blackout shades in your room if the sun wakes you every morning before the alarm clock does. Try to be be in bed before 10 pm.

Use Your Happiest Memories To Change Your Current State

I interviewed the wonderful Rabbi Zelig Pliskin of Jerusalem for this book. He gave me this jewel from his book, *Conversations With Yourself.* Tell yourself:
"I consistently access positive states."
"My awesome brain stores all my best states. Which state do I want to choose now?"(Whenever you experience a great state give it a unique name. This way you will be able to access that memory from your personal library of great states.)" So when you feel down, think back to your happiest memories. This will put you into a positive and happier state.

Tame Your Critical Voice

I asked the ebullient author of *Happy 4 Life*, Dr. Bob Nozik for advice for this book. He recommends that you turn your inner critic into an inner colleague. First, here it speak to you. Listen to it, and then stop it. Never let it talk to you in a way that is rude. Eventually it will speak to you humorously and helpfully. You need your inner voice to help organize your life but it doesn't have to be mean to you.

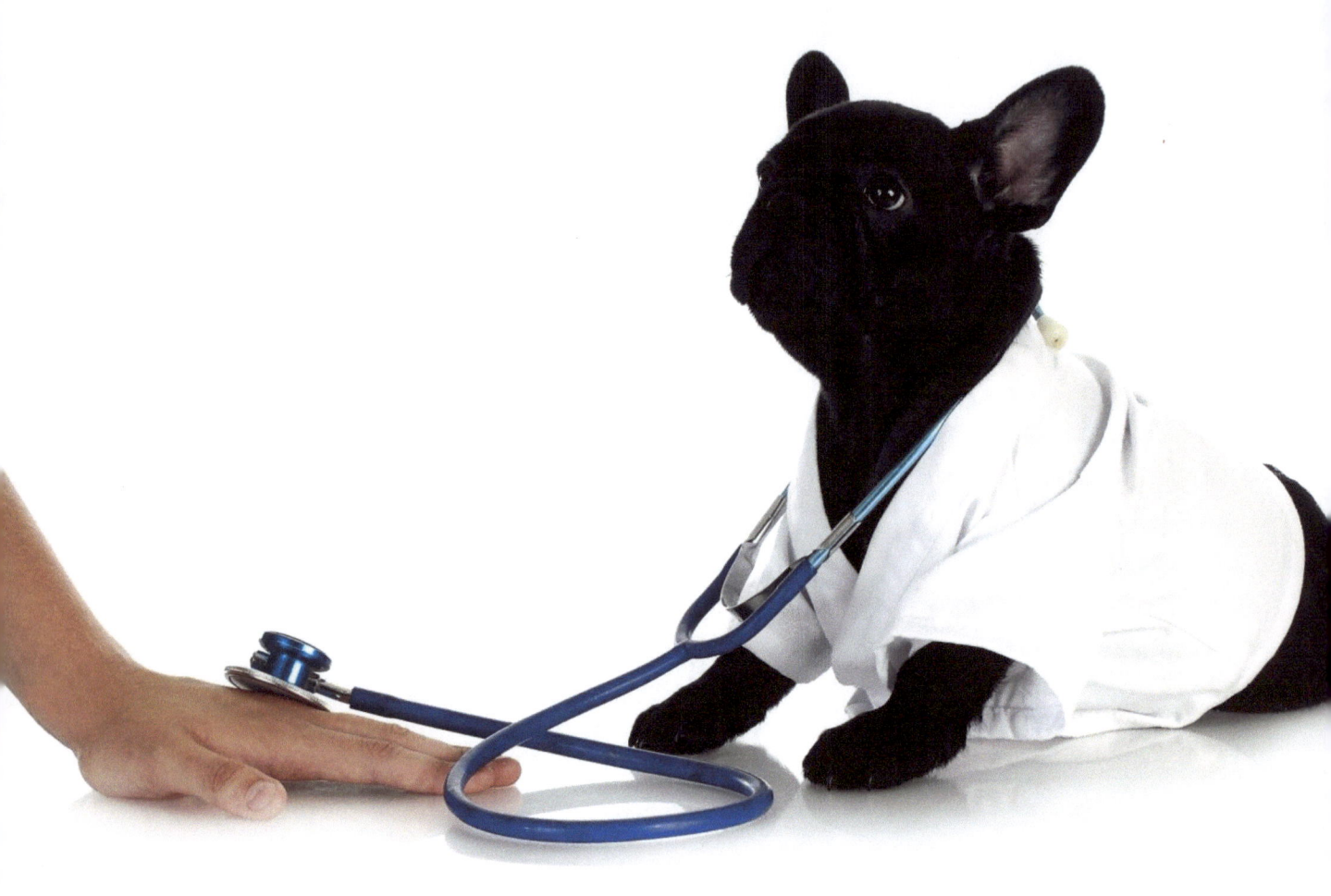

Get A Career

We spend most of our waking hours at work. Don't settle for just a job. Find a career that you are passionate about. Move to a different city if you have to. When you do something that you love, and it is a noble pursuit, you are fulfilling your purpose.

Memorize Two Great Jokes

Jokes are a great icebreaker when you meet new people. If you don't have a good memory, put them on your smartphone. They can also be used to lighten a tense situation. Why two jokes? The first joke is a warm-up. When everyone is laughing, you can raise the fun in the room with the second. Keep it clean and inoffensive.

Come Up With A Great Idea

Think about ways to improve humanity. It could be an invention, a service, or a way to make an existing process better. Once you have that idea in mind, do something about it. I know someone who works with inventors. He said the worst thing you can do is keep your inventions to yourself. This idea could become your purpose and inspire you to get out of bed every morning and have a successful day. It's also a good idea to keep your dog away from your laptop.

Compliment People Often

Encouragement is the invisible energy that helps drive people forward and higher. Kind words can change a person's day for the better, and could also change their life. I remember some compliments that people gave me years ago.

Find The Right Thing To Focus On

Lionel Ketchian, the author of *Happiness Formula* and a Happiness Hall Of Fame inductee suggests, "What you focus on expands. If you focus on the negative, you will experience more negativity in your life. Happiness is the most important thing to focus your life on. Happiness is an inner state of well-being that enables you to profit from your highest thoughts, intelligence, wisdom, awareness, common sense, emotions, health, and spiritual values."

Give

It doesn't matter if you don't have a lot of money. You can give your time. Give sincere compliments to people daily. Understand that as you are giving, you are gaining. You are contributing to the betterment of the universe.

Ask Yourself Great Questions

Instead of asking yourself what would be the most decadent thing to eat when you are at a restaurant, ask yourself what would be the healthiest thing to eat that will keep you energized and fully engaged. When confronted with a choice, ask yourself if your decision will get you closer to your goal or push you further away. Instead of asking yourself "Can I?" ask yourself, "How can I?"

Meditate

Father Alapaki Kim is considered to be the Mother Theresa of Hawaii. For a dozen years he lived in squalor with rats running across his face every night, so he could be close to and serve Hawaii's poor. I asked him over breakfast how an ordinary man can increase his happiness. He said, "Meditate. In meditation you get to know yourself. The more you know yourself; you will know that God resides within us. That will give you joy. The more you see God in you, the more you will see God in others. You will be able to serve people that are difficult, even people that want to harm you or hurt you."

Be Open To Love

My wonderful father, Michael J. Duffy, wrote, "Love is the center point of living." Love is why we are here. Loving others is great karma. What you send out, you will receive back many times over. Leave a legacy of love. Don't waste your time on this earth worried about getting your little heart broken. Be bold and accept the fact that you will get hurt from time to time. You will also be greatly rewarded. Love all races, faiths, and people. We are all God's children. Love deeply, bravely, and profoundly.

Credits

Conversations with Yourself. Author Zelig Pliskin Publisher: Mesorah Pubns Ltd (January 1, 2007)

All of the wonderful photos are from 123 RF.com. A great thank you to the following artists:
John McAllister© *123RF.com*
Robert Neumann© *123RF.com*
Ewastudio© *123RF.com*
Tatiana Katsia© *123RF.com*
Daniela Jakob© *123RF.com*
Bruno Coimbra© *123RF.com*
Aaron Amat© *123RF.com*
Kitch Bain© *123RF.com*
Judith Dzierzawa© *123RF.com*
Piyagoon Panyo© *123RF.com*
Wisiel© *123RF.com*
Tobkatrina© *123RF.com*
Eric Isselee© *123RF.com*

Acknowledgements

I would like to thank all of the people that have shared their wisdom with me including: Dr. Fred Luskin, Dr. Laura Delizonna, Tal Ben-Shahar, Shawn Achor, Dan Gilbert, Fr. Alapaki Kim, Deepak Chopra and Zelig Pliskin.

About the Author

Mike Duffy is the founder of Happiness Publishing, LLC. He has been researching happiness for over 29 years. He is the author of *The Happiness Book For Kids: A Child's Guide To Happiness! Volume I & II* and *The Happiness Book For Little Christians: A Biblical Guide To Happiness!* He loves to speak about how you can gain greater happiness and joy in your wonderful and precious life. His audiences include corporations, universities and organizations. Mike is the founder of The Happiness Hall Of Fame. The Happiness Hall of Fame recognizes, encourages and celebrates people that through their talent, hard work and sacrifice make other people happy.
www.happinesshalloffame.com

www.ingramcontent.com/pod-product-compliance
Lightning Source LLC
Chambersburg PA
CBHW041700160426
43191CB00002B/31